4 READING

a 1 A manager   2 The afternoon
3 A pedestrian   4 Laptops
5 An antique shop   6 Your boss
7 Eating   8 A friend

PRACTICAL ENGLISH 1

1 AT IMMIGRATION

1 travelling   2 in   3 purpose   4 holiday
5 long   6 Where   7 with   8 Is   9 it's
10 enjoy

2 SOCIAL ENGLISH

No, thanks, I'm fine. Shall we go?   8
Long! 12 hours.   4
Great! Let's go then.   10
I'm fine.   2
No, I'm OK. I always sleep on planes.   6
How was the flight?   3
Sure. My car's outside in the car park.   9
Wow, you must be really tired.   5
Hello, Tom. How are you?   1
Would you like a coffee or anything?   7

3 READING

b 1 San Francisco Bay to the north and
east, the Pacific Ocean to the west.
2 No, the best way to explore is on foot.
3 South Market and the Mission District.
4 Prices are higher, queues are longer
and (finding a) parking (space) is
impossible.
5 October

2A

1 VOCABULARY

a 1 go swimming/sailing   2 go abroad
3 go camping   4 take photos
5 buy souvenirs   6 hire a car
7 go out at night   8 go for a walk
9 stay in a hotel   10 go sightseeing

b 1 freezing   2 boiling   3 snow   4 foggy
5 cloudy   6 rain

2 GRAMMAR

a **Regular:** arrived, remembered, talked,
stayed, hated, walked, argued

Irregular: became, began, broke, did,
had, spent, saw

b 1 We didn't study in Korea.
2 They didn't speak Russian.
3 My uncle wasn't a doctor.
4 I didn't sleep well.
5 My mum didn't enjoy the film.
6 He didn't pick up the receipt.
7 You weren't on time.

c 1 went   2 flew   3 rented   4 drove
5 had   6 didn't know   7 were
8 argued

d 1 Where did they fly to?
2 When did they go there?
3 Did they have a good time?
4 Did they get on well?
5 How many times did they argue?

3 PRONUNCIATION

a 1 needed   2 wanted   3 loved
4 waited

b /ɔː/ caught, bought, saw
/e/ read, said, went
/əʊ/ wrote, broke, drove
/æ/ rang, drank, sat
/eɪ/ came, gave, made

2B

1 GRAMMAR

a 1 was sleeping   2 were you talking
3 wasn't working   4 were living
5 were you watching   6 were walking
7 wasn't driving   8 was snowing

b 1 They were playing tennis when it
started to rain.
2 He broke his leg when he was skiing.
3 The boys were fighting when their
father came home.
4 A dog ate my sandwich when I was
sleeping in the park.
5 We were studying in the library
when the fire started.

c 1 went   2 were having   3 got
4 was speaking   5 noticed
6 was sitting   7 decided   8 went
9 said   10 stopped   11 was passing
12 took   13 came   14 was smiling
15 looked   16 was laughing

2 VOCABULARY

a 1 at   2 in   3 In, on, on   4 in   5 in
6 on, in   7 in, in   8 at, on

b 1 at   2 at, in, at   3 on, in, at, on
4 on, –   5 on   6 in   7 on, in
8 At, in, in

3 PRONUNCIATION

a/b 1 fam(ou)s   2 simil(ar)   3 lat(er)
4 nation(a)l   5 dr(a)matic   6 phot(o)graph
7 gard(e)n   8 memor(a)ble   9 wom(a)n

5 Which   6 How many   7 How long
8 What   9 What   10 Why

2 GRAMMAR

a 1 a   2 b   3 a   4 b   5 a   6 a

b 1–3   2–5   3–6   4–4   5–1   6–2

c 1 Who painted *The Last Supper*?
2 When did Kurt Cobain die?
3 Where do penguins live?
4 How many Oscars did *The Lord of
the Rings* win in 2004?
5 Who won the Oscar for Best Director?
6 Where was Maria Sharapova born?
7 When did your brother go to
New York?

3 PRONUNCIATION

a walk, wash, quickly, white, one

b who, hair, happy, hands

2D

1 GRAMMAR

a 1 really mean   2 snowing   3 can't
4 a bit expensive   5 don't like him

b 1 because, d   2 so, e   3 because, f
4 so, c   5 so, b   6 because, a

c 1 because, so, Although
2 because, so, Although
3 but, Although, so

2 VOCABULARY

a 1 d   2 g   3 f   4 b   5 a   6 e   7 c

3 PRONUNCIATION

/æ/ accident
/eɪ/ date
/ɔː/ awful
/ɑː/ dance
/ə/ woman

4 READING

a 5, 1, 4, 3, 2

CAN YOU REMEMBER...?

1 do   2 doesn't   3 are   4 who   5 did
6 were   7 wrote   8 Although

PRACTICAL ENGLISH 2

1 CALLING RECEPTION

1 This is room 724.
2 My room is very cold.
3 There's a problem with the heating.
4 The air-conditioning isn't working.
5 Can I have a chicken sandwich, please?
6 Do you have any fresh fruit juice?

2 SOCIAL ENGLISH

1 well, c   2 How, d   3 What, for, a
4 This, e   5 time, b

3 READING

1 T   2 T   3 T   4 ?   5 T   6 F   7 ?   8 F

A

1 GRAMMAR

a 1 're going to play
2 isn't going to rain
3 are you going to put
4 isn't going to jump
5 are they going to stay
6 'm going to buy
7 aren't going to eat
8 Are you going to shave

b 1 're going   2 'm taking   3 're climbing
4 aren't windsurfing   5 're having
6 're going   7 'm planning

c 1 I'm going to pass
2 I'm going to spend / I'm spending
3 it's going to be
4 He's going to have / He's having
5 We're not going to miss
6 are you going
7 It's going to be
8 she's going to have

2 VOCABULARY

1 I'm looking for
2 I'm looking forward to
3 I'm looking after
4 I'm looking after
5 I'm looking for
6 I'm looking forward to
7 I'm looking for
8 I'm looking forward to
9 I'm looking after

3 PRONUNCIATION

a /ʌ/ money, month
/əʊ/ own, hotel
/uː/ improve, honeymoon

B

1 GRAMMAR

1 'll snow, 'll rain   2 'll be
3 won't finish, 'll be   4 won't pass
5 'll be able to, 'll need

2 VOCABULARY

1 lose   2 fail   3 forgot   4 leave   5 teach
6 turn off   7 sent   8 borrow   9 found
10 pull

3 PRONUNCIATION

a /ɒ/ enjoy
/əʊ/ stop
/ɒ/ work
/əʊ/ problem

4 READING

a 1 Cancer   2 No, they won't.
3 Buy any new clothes.   4 Aquarius
5 Taurus   6 Pisces

C

1 PRONUNCIATION

a 1 receive   2 forget   3 arrive   4 repair
5 exist   6 address

2 GRAMMAR

a 1 I think I'll go to bed.
2 Shall I turn off the air-conditioning?
3 I won't drive fast.
4 I'll buy (you) another one.
5 Shall I call the police?
6 I'll have the chicken.

b 1 P   2 D   3 O   4 O   5 P   6 D

3 VOCABULARY

1 come   2 call   3 pay   4 drive
5 give   6 take

4 READING

a 4, 6, 2, 5, 1, 3, 8, 7

D

1 GRAMMAR

a 1 did, dream, was running, was,
was flying
2 Do, dream, have
3 Are, doing, 'm having, Do, want
4 are, doing, 're practising

b 1 are, going to do   2 Are, going to
watch   3 did, do   4 spends   5 makes
6 watch   7 does, do / is, doing
8 don't eat   9 eat   10 did, have
11 turn on   12 will, be

c 1 I'm going to   2 I'll   3 I'm going to
4 I'm going to   5 I'll   6 I'll

2 PRONUNCIATION

a 1 meeting   2 patient   3 champagne
4 successful   5 violin   6 tomorrow
7 optimistic   8 psychoanalyst
9 understanding

3 VOCABULARY

1 to   2 about   3 to   4 with   5 about
6 for   7 with   8 to

CAN YOU REMEMBER...?

1 didn't   2 took   3 Which   4 which
5 going   6 won't   7 Shall   8 is

PRACTICAL ENGLISH 3

1 PROBLEMS WITH A MEAL

1 here, table   4 rare, done
2 dirty, have   5 mistake, any
3 cold, for

2 SOCIAL ENGLISH

We could go to a little café that I know. 5
Listen, it's still early. Shall we go for a
walk? 3
Thank you. That was a lovely dinner. 1
That sounds great. We could have another
coffee. 6
Good idea. Where shall we go? 4
You're very welcome. I'm glad you
enjoyed it. 2

3 READING

a 1 ?   2 T   3 T   4 T   5 F   6 ?
7 ?   8 F

4A

1 VOCABULARY

a **Across:** 2 dress   5 jacket   6 suit
7 socks   10 tights   11 tie   12 jeans
13 top

Down: 1 tracksuit   3 trousers   4 hat
7 shirt   8 shoes   9 belt

b 1 gets dressed   2 wear   3 try on
4 put on   5 Take off

2 PRONUNCIATION

/ʃ/ shirt, shoes, shorts
/t/ trousers, top, tie
/s/ socks, dress, suit
/k/ skirt, cap, coat

3 GRAMMAR

a 1 He hasn't been to London.
2 She's broken her leg.
3 Have they eaten there before?
4 Have you tried ice-skating?
5 I haven't seen this film.
6 We've had an argument.
7 Have you ever lost your ID card?
8 He hasn't met her parents.

b 1 never   2 ever   3 never   4 ever
5 never   6 ever   7 ever   8 never

c 1 Have you ever worn, have, did you
wear, went
2 Have you ever borrowed, have, did
you borrow, needed
3 Have you ever met, haven't
4 Have you ever bought, have, bought
5 Have you ever had, have, took,
ruined

4B

1 VOCABULARY

1 tidy   2 make   3 do   4 change   5 use
6 take   7 spend   8 clean

2 GRAMMAR

a 1 I've already washed the floor.
2 Have you seen this film yet?
3 Daniel has already made his bed.
4 My parents haven't learnt to use the
Internet yet.
5 You've already made a mistake.
6 We've already been to New York.
7 Has the film started yet?
8 Edward has already found a new job.

b 1 's just fallen   2 's just done
3 've just won   4 've just woken up
5 've just bought   6 've just missed

3 PRONUNCIATION

1 yellow   2 yesterday   3 year
4 university   5 young
6 January, June, July   7 jacket   8 jeans
9 generous   10 judo

4 READING

a 1 T   2 F   3 F   4 F   5 T   6 F

4C

1 GRAMMAR

a 1 worse   2 more slowly   3 harder
4 more stressful   5 funnier   6 wetter
7 better   8 more popular

b 1 isn't as quiet as this one
2 doesn't speak as quickly as Carlos
3 isn't as big as Russia
4 didn't play as well as Portugal
5 doesn't drive as carefully as Davina
6 isn't as expensive as Tokyo
7 doesn't dress as elegantly as Ivana
8 isn't as relaxing as classical music

2 PRONUNCIATION

a/b 1 ago   2 future   3 parents
4 happened   5 American   6 harder
7 generation   8 machines
9 journalist   10 today   11 sickness
12 longer

3 VOCABULARY

1 waste   2 take a long
3 don't have enough   4 spend
5 save   6 on

4 READING

a A 3   B 1   C 4   D 5   E 2
b 1 F   2 T   3 T   4 F   5 F   6 T

4D

1 GRAMMAR

a 1 most polluted   2 most impatient
3 furthest   4 cheapest   5 easiest
6 worst   7 most dangerous
8 most boring

b 1 busiest   2 dirtiest   3 more expensive
4 noisiest   5 slower

c 1 He's the rudest person I've ever met.
2 This is the most exciting book I've
ever read.
3 It's the most beautiful building we've
ever seen.
4 That's the funniest joke you've ever
told.
5 It's the most beautiful photograph
I've ever taken.
6 That's the stupidest thing I've ever
done.
7 That's the most delicious meal she's
ever made.
8 These are the best poems he's ever
written.

2 VOCABULARY

a 1 interesting   2 impatient   3 safe
4 noisy   5 rude   6 crowded
7 polluted   8 modern

b 1 unhealthy   2 impossible
3 uncomfortable   4 unfriendly
5 impolite   6 unhappy   7 untidy
8 impatient

3 PRONUNCIATION

a /ɔː/ dirty
/ɜː/ bought
/əʊ/ world
/ɔː/ Rome

b 1 unfriendly   2 beautiful   3 exciting
4 dangerous   5 dishonest   6 unhappy
7 unhealthy   8 impossible

CAN YOU REMEMBER...?

1 going   2 will   3 won't   4 Does   5 Has
6 have   7 as   8 ever

PRACTICAL ENGLISH 4

1 ASKING FOR INFORMATION

1 a   2 is   3 far   4 near   5 Can   6 take
7 on   8 on   9 close   10 until

2 SOCIAL ENGLISH

1 know   2 think   3 sure   4 remember
5 right   6 doing   7 studying   8 holiday
9 where   10 kind

3 READING

a 1 14 miles   2 $12   3 $4   4 $44
5 5.30 a.m.   6 taxi, airport bus

5 A

1 GRAMMAR

a 1 not to have   2 to meet
3 not to worry   4 to close   5 not to tell
6 to relax   7 to take

b 1 important to be
2 careful not to drop
3 dangerous to swim
4 difficult to sleep
5 interesting to talk to
6 nice to see
7 easy to use

c 1 to study   2 to learn   3 to buy
4 to have   5 to make   6 to take
7 to argue   8 to meet

2 VOCABULARY

I'm Bill. I'm 16 and I've decided **to** leave
school. I'm going **to** leave next week. I'm
hoping **to** get a job with computers
because I'm planning **to** make lots of
money.

I've tried **to** work hard but I'm not a very
good student. All the other students
understand and learn **to** do things quickly
but not me. And I never remember **to**
bring my books to class and always forget
to do my homework.

I'd like **to** learn **to** fly because I want **to** be
a pilot. But first I need **to** do a course. My
mother offered **to** pay for the course but
only if I promised **to** finish school!

3 PRONUNCIATION

a 1 re<u>mem</u>ber   2 re<u>cep</u>tion   3 sur<u>vive</u>
4 de<u>cide</u>   5 pre<u>tend</u>   6 to<u>mor</u>row
7 ad<u>vice</u>   8 es<u>cape</u>

4 READING

a 1 F   2 F   3 T   4 F   5 T   6 T

5 B

1 GRAMMAR

a 1 tidying   2 going   3 making
4 eating   5 talking   6 travelling

b 1 c   2 a   3 e   4 f   5 d   6 b

c 1 Writing   2 sending   3 imagining
4 driving   5 listening   6 Staying
7 reading   8 getting up   9 taking
10 going   11 getting   12 having
13 Turning   14 leaving

d 1 to get   2 to stop   3 working
4 to set up   5 cooking   6 to open
7 to spend   8 learning   9 getting up
10 catching   11 travelling   12 working
13 sailing   14 surfing   15 to move
16 teaching   17 to be

2 PRONUNCIATION

a 1 <u>sing</u>ing   2 <u>lang</u>uage   3 <u>mor</u>ning
4 <u>lis</u>tening   5 en<u>joy</u>ing   6 re<u>lax</u>ing
7 re<u>mem</u>bering   8 pre<u>tend</u>ing

3 VOCABULARY

1 c   2 d   3 f   4 a   5 e   6 b

5 C

1 GRAMMAR

a 1 have to   2 don't have to
3 doesn't have to   4 has to   5 have to
6 don't have to   7 Does, have to, have to
8 Does, have to, have to

b 1 You must fasten your safety belt.
2 You must stop here.
3 You mustn't smoke.
4 You must turn left.
5 You must wear a helmet.
6 You mustn't walk on the grass.

c 1 don't have to   2 mustn't
3 don't have to   4 mustn't   5 mustn't
6 don't have to

2 PRONUNCIATION

a 1 mus⫶n't   2 lis⫶en   3 ha⫶f
4 We⫶nesday   5 ⫶nees   6 ⫶now
7 w⫶ile   8 si⫶n   8 wa⫶k

3 VOCABULARY

1 British and American English are very
similar.
2 English pronunciation can be quite
difficult.
3 Learning Japanese isn't very easy.
4 I think Hungarian is incredibly
complicated.
5 Czech is a bit easier.
6 Reading is a really useful way to learn
vocabulary.

4 READING

b 1 Ana   2 Péter, Sompong   3 Konrad
4 Elke   5 Péter

5 D

1 VOCABULARY

a 1 football   2 baseball   3 swimming
4 skiing   5 volleyball   6 tennis
7 rugby   8 aerobics   9 cycling
10 golf

b 1 play   2 go   3 plays   4 go
5 does   6 play

c 1 skiing   2 baseball   3 basketball
4 volleyball   5 swimming

d 1 down   2 round   3 through
4 over   5 through

2 GRAMMAR

a 1 is running across   2 is going through
3 is cycling up   4 are skiing down
5 is getting out of   6 are rowing round

b 1 round   2 out of   3 to   4 into
5 along   6 under   7 past   8 through
9 along   10 towards   11 across

3 PRONUNCIATION

/ɒ/ over
/ə/ through
/aʊ/ under

CAN YOU REMEMBER...?

1 been   2 hasn't   3 more   4 most   5 to
6 doing   7 mustn't   8 out

PRACTICAL ENGLISH 5

1 TAKING SOMETHING BACK

1 bought   2 decided   3 tried   4 too
5 refund   6 here

2 SOCIAL ENGLISH

1 What, think   2 Never   3 lovely
4 would, like   5 good, idea   6 lost

3 READING

a 1 latest   2 boutiques   3 overlooks
4 won't break the bank   5 crowds
6 huge

b 1 Borders   2 Borders
3 Banana Republic   4 Virgin Megastore
5 Camper   6 Borders

6 A

1 GRAMMAR

a 1 c 2 a 3 f 4 b 5 e 6 d

b 1 take 2 will break 3 hear 4 stay
5 will be 6 see 7 'll get 8 will feel

c 1 D 2 C 3 F 4 A 5 G 6 B 7 E

d 1 puts, will come
2 see, will have
3 walk, will have
4 throw, make, will come
5 dig, will find
6 break, will have
7 flies, will have, kill, will have, will be

2 VOCABULARY

1 wearing, carrying 2 won, earned
3 say, told 4 hoping, waited
5 watched, look at 6 known, met
7 make, do 8 look, look, look like

3 PRONUNCIATION

a 1 b 2 e 3 f 4 c 5 a 6 d

6 B

1 GRAMMAR

a 1 had, would drive
2 saw, would be
3 wouldn't know, found
4 would, do, lost
5 were, would come
6 would buy, had

b 1 If I saw a shark, I'd be very
frightened.
2 What would you do if you saw a fire?
3 He'd go sailing if he could swim.
4 If she won the lottery, she'd buy lots
of new clothes.
5 What would people do if they
couldn't watch TV?
6 I'd go to the doctor's if I were you.

2 PRONUNCIATION

a 1 open, chicken, insect
2 about, afraid, attack
3 finally, animal, crocodile
4 direction, mosquito, safari

3 VOCABULARY

Across: 1 bear 3 tiger 4 elephant
7 sheep

Down: 1 butterfly 2 lion 3 eagle
6 horse

4 READING

b Sentence 2

6 C

1 GRAMMAR

a 1 might go 2 might get
3 might continue 4 might rent
5 might live 6 might share
7 might not want 8 might fail
9 might have to

b 1 might 2 may not 3 might
4 might 5 may not 6 might 7 might
8 may not

2 PRONUNCIATION

a 1 organization 2 invitation 3 election
4 information 5 imagination
6 translation 7 communication
8 decision

3 VOCABULARY

a **Verb:** communicate, conclude, correct,
confuse, demonstrate, inject, organize,
predict

Noun: communication, conclusion,
correction, confusion, demonstration,
injection, organization, prediction

b 1 conclusion 2 communicate
3 injection 4 demonstration
5 prediction 6 organize

4 READING

a 1 T 2 F 3 T 4 F 5 T 6 T
7 F 8 T

6 D

1 GRAMMAR

a 1 should, B
2 should, F
3 shouldn't, A
4 shouldn't, E
5 shouldn't, D
6 should, C

b 1 should tell 2 shouldn't be
3 shouldn't go 4 should go
5 should buy 6 should join
7 shouldn't watch

c 1 D 2 F 3 A 4 B 5 C 6 G 7 E

2 PRONUNCIATION

a 1 would 2 should 3 could
4 understood 5 good

3 VOCABULARY

1 getting, worse 2 got, e-mails
3 get, angry 4 get, tickets 5 get, on
6 gets, home 7 get, married
8 is getting, taller 9 'm getting, off
10 got, lost

CAN YOU REMEMBER...?

1 to 2 having 3 don't 4 through
5 won't 6 would 7 might / may
8 should

PRACTICAL ENGLISH 6

1 ASKING FOR MEDICINE

1 help 2 hurts 3 have 4 Are 5 think
6 might 7 take 8 times 9 often
10 much

2 SOCIAL ENGLISH

1 Bless
2 How, sounds, shall, mind, choose
3 sorry, pity

3 READING

a 1 You must keep this medicine
somewhere safe.
2 You should be careful not to take too
much of this medicine.
3 You have to turn your mobile off.
4 You should be careful with your
belongings.
5 You mustn't smoke here.
6 You should be careful or you might
fall over.
7 You shouldn't leave anything valuable
in your car.
8 You shouldn't drink this water.
9 You must make sure that the door is
never left open.
10 You should be very careful if you're
driving here.
11 You have to wait until a waiter shows
you where to sit.
12 You mustn't use radios in this park.

7 A

1 VOCABULARY

1 frightened 2 terrified 3 wasps, spiders
4 panic 5 closed spaces 6 heights

2 GRAMMAR

a 1 since 2 for 3 for 4 since
5 Since, for 6 since 7 since
8 For, since

b 1 since 2 for 3 since 4 for 5 for
6 since 7 for 8 for 9 since 10 since

c 1 How long have, lived
2 When did, move out
3 How long have, been
4 How long has, been
5 When did, become
6 How long has, been
7 When did, get

d 1 Gill *has lived* here for seven years.
2 How long *has she been* a professional dancer?
3 They *have been married* since 2000.
4 He has been in France *since* February.
5 How long *have you had* your car?
6 He's had this job *for* eight years.
7 She *has had* three homes since she was born.
8 My parents *lived / have lived* in the same house for many years.

3 PRONUNCIATION

a 1 /ɪ/ 2 /ɪ/ 3 /aɪ/ 4 /aɪ/ 5 /aɪ/ 6 /ɪ/
7 /aɪ/ 8 /ɪ/

1 VOCABULARY

1 c 2 d 3 g 4 e 5 b 6 h 7 f 8 a

2 PRONUNCIATION

a **Stress on 2nd syllable:** suc<u>cess</u>ful, ca<u>reer</u>, ap<u>pear</u>, di<u>rect</u>, di<u>rect</u>or
Stress on 1st syllable: <u>fa</u>mous, <u>cin</u>ema, <u>vio</u>lence, <u>tic</u>ket, <u>ac</u>tor

3 GRAMMAR

a 1 've known 2 were 3 met 4 were
5 've been 6 went 7 were 8 chose
9 told 10 've been 11 've shared

b 1 have, lived 2 got, were
3 left, 've worked 4 did, go, took
5 have, had, bought
6 haven't seen, moved

4 READING

a 1, 6, 3, 7, 5, 4, 2

b 1 was 2 did his family move
3 did he see 4 did he work
5 has he been married

c 1 In 1941. / On January 5, 1941.
2 In 1952.
3 (When he was) at secondary school.
4 For eight years (from 1963 to 1971).
5 For 40 years. / Since 1965.

1 GRAMMAR

a 1 Did you use to enjoy
2 didn't use to like
3 used to be
4 Did Colin use to work
5 didn't use to be
6 used to live
7 didn't use to do
8 Did he use to play

b 1 used 2 used to 3 didn't use to
4 Did you use to 5 used
6 Did your children use to

2 PRONUNCIATION

a /z/ used to
/s/ friends
/tʃ/ school
/dʒ/ great

3 VOCABULARY

1 c 2 g 3 e 4 b 5 a 6 f 7 h 8 d

4 READING

a 1 Where did you go to school?
2 Did you ever get into trouble?
3 What subjects were you good at?
4 Did you have a favourite teacher?
5 What did you want to do when you were young?
6 What's the most important lesson you've learned in life?

b 1 T 2 ? 3 F 4 ? 5 T 6 F
7 F 8 T

1 GRAMMAR

a 1 Aspirin is used to relieve pain.
2 The sandwich was named after the Earl of Sandwich.
3 St Paul's Cathedral was designed by Christopher Wren.
4 This film is based on a true story.
5 The first crossword puzzle was published in 1913.
6 The first credit card was issued by the Diner's Club.
7 The fax machine is not used very often these days.
8 Penicillin was discovered by Alexander Fleming.

b 1 President Kennedy was assassinated in 1963.
2 Champagne is made in France.
3 What is your dog called?
4 Television was invented by John Logie Baird.
5 This room is cleaned every morning.
6 Her flat was designed by a famous architect.
7 Stamps are only sold in the Post Office.
8 Where were those shoes made?

c 1 I was stopped by the police last night.
2 *Crocodile Rock* was sung by Elton John.
3 All the photographs at our wedding were taken by my cousin.
4 The heating is controlled by a computer.
5 The first World Cup was won by Uruguay.
6 This wasn't painted by Van Gogh!
7 Was the telephone invented by Edison?

2 VOCABULARY

1 designed 2 named 3 discovered
4 used 5 created 6 invented 7 made
8 recorded 9 written 10 based

3 PRONUNCIATION

a /d/ painted, based
/ɪd/ checked, rained
/t/ discovered

CAN YOU REMEMBER...?

1 have 2 were 3 not 4 shouldn't
5 long 6 did 7 used 8 were

PRACTICAL ENGLISH 7

1 BUYING TICKETS

Return, please. How much is that? 3
Thanks. Oh, can I get anything to eat on the train? 9
Can I have a ticket to Glasgow, please? 1
Good. And what time does it arrive? 7
Here you are. When does the next train leave? 5
That's £15.80. 4
It gets there at 12.15. 8
Yes, there's a trolley service with snacks and drinks. 10
In ten minutes. 6
Single or return? 2

2 SOCIAL ENGLISH

1 looking 2 take, ready
3 Why, wondered